T0160923

SOMETHING CROSSES MY MIND

SOMETHING CROSSES MY MIND
有什么在我心里一过

Selected Poetry of
Wang Xiaoni
王小妮

Translated from Chinese by **Eleanor Goodman**

Zephyr Press & The Chinese University Press of Hong Kong
Brookline, Mass | Hong Kong

Cover image by Xu Bing
Book design by *type*slowly
Printed in Hong Kong

Acknowledgments:

"Moonlight Is Very White," "Thinking That, Then Thinking This," "Those I Don't Know I Don't Want to Know," "Early Morning," "Starting Anew as a Poet," *Pathlight* issue 3 (Summer 2012); "Going Out to Plant Sunflowers," "Plowman," "Religious Sheep," *World Literature Today*, vol. 87, no. 5 (Aug. 2013); "The One Lifting a Lamp in Front of the Mud Hut," "Typhoon, No. 2," *Little Star* mobile app (Feb. 2014); "Silent All the Way from Beijing to Guangzhou," "The One Holding Peanuts," "Thoughts Upon Crossing Guangxi," *Pleiades* (Spring 2014); "Meeting Death's Envoy on a Winter Afternoon," "Moonlight, No. 1," "Moonlight, No. 2," "Moonlight, No. 3," *Asymptote* (July 2014)

This publication is supported by the Jintian Literary Foundation.
Zephyr Press also acknowledges with gratitude the financial support
of the Massachusetts Cultural Council.

massculturalcouncil.org

Zephyr Press, a non-profit arts and education 501(c)(3) organization,
publishes literary titles that foster a deeper understanding of cultures
and languages. Zephyr Press books are distributed to the trade in the U.S.
and Canada by Consortium Book Sales and Distribution [www.cbsd.com]
and by Small Press Distribution [www.spdbooks.org].

Published for the rest of the world by:
The Chinese University Press
The Chinese University of Hong Kong
Sha Tin, N.T., Hong Kong

Cataloguing-in publication data is available from the Library of Congress.

ZEPHYR PRESS
www.zephyrpress.org

JINTIAN
www.jintian.net

THE CHINESE UNIVERSITY PRESS
www.chineseupress.com

CONTENTS

Translator's Foreword

In the world of contemporary Chinese poetry, Wang Xiaoni's work cannot be neatly fit into any of the most fashionable categories. She does not write avant-garde absurdism nor highly intellectualized verse. She does not experiment with the prose poem, conversational style, previously verboten sexual content, or highly wrought symbolism. She rarely uses the internet as a platform for her poetry. She is not interested in imitating T.S. Eliot or Li Bai.

Her poems seem to spring from direct observation that is then transfigured. For Wang Xiaoni metaphors tend to be the bones on which the flesh of her poems are hung. This, along with her interest in social issues and her complete lack of reliance on personal confession, gives her a unique voice among her contemporaries.

Wang Xiaoni was born in 1955 in Jilin not far from the North Korean border and she lived through the entirety of the Cultural Revolution. She was in the first group of young people to go to college after Mao Zedong's death, and there she became involved in the university poetry club, quickly establishing herself as one of the leading voices of her generation. Her quiet but powerful verse became much admired in the excitement of the 1980s, which saw a sudden opening up of intellectual and creative floodgates. She was among the first, and one of the few women, to ride those waves.

Wang Xiaoni might be considered a poet of place—she is distinctly a northerner writing in a southern clime, and notices details that locals might overlook. In 1985, a few years after graduating from college, she moved across the country to Shenzhen, a southern city bordering Hong Kong's New Territories. The accompanying sense of dislocation, and of her outsider status, still carries through her poetry. The speakers in her poems can be overwhelmed by a basket of potatoes (a northern staple), and there is a kind of distance or alienation in the descriptions of banana trees and cicadas, the typhoons with their "herds of black cattle," and the southern scarecrows, which become "the only living things." This acute awareness of the environment writ large is one of the sources of her power as a poet.

Yet she is also a poet of the in-between spaces, the distances traveled between here and somewhere else, physically, psychologically, and sociologically. Many of her poems take place on trains, airplanes, or buses, or in other nominal spaces.

> There must be someone who stays awake.
> There must be someone who understands
> only then will the train agree to run from Beijing to Guangzhou.
>
> Such a long journey
> enough to cut across five small countries
> to startle awake five governors dozing in their gardens.
> But a Chinese train
> is like a peasant burrowing his way through a cornfield.
> —"Silent All the Way from Beijing to Guangzhou"

There is a wonderful whimsicality in the five governors being disturbed from their naps, and in the image of the train as a peasant. But more important to understanding Wang Xiaoni's style is the sense of isolation in the midst of collectivity seen in the first stanza. This is a common theme that runs through much of Wang's work, a kind of deliberate passivity or silence that then finds release on the page. Later in the poem, she writes "On Chinese trains / I don't say a thing." In her ordinary life, the poet observes but does not comment. Life becomes material in the strictest sense; it is something to be used to create something else, namely art. The speaker isolates herself in order to move closer to the deeper truth: "Each day from morning to night / the door is shut tight. / I hang the sun at the angle I need it." And when this small, tightly controlled world is violated, even in the smallest way, the poet's psyche rebels.

I hadn't expected
after I wiped the glass clean
the entire world would immediately infiltrate in.
The last shelter disappeared with the water
even the leaves thickened their eyebrows
to spy in.

I hadn't thought
such a mistake could be made
with only two hours of work and a rag.

Every thing is a master of betrayal.
This most ancient craftsmanship
was easily accomplished by a soft dirty rag.
Now I'm stranded in the midst of its exposure.
                              —"A Rag's Betrayal"

Perhaps it is poets most of the world who require the most protection from it. Wang Xiaoni is nothing if not grounded in China—its people, its fauna and flora, its politics. Yet to have that world look in on her is a nightmare. Even more, it is a betrayal of the compact the poet has made with the world: to live in it as a stranger, but to give it full life on the page. This agreement at times infuses Wang's work with an almost mystical sense of estrangement.

That is not to say that Wang Xiaoni is a poet with her head in the stars. Rather, she is grounded in the earth: she writes of potatoes and peanuts, scarecrows and corn. The animals in her poems are water buffalo, pigs and sheep. What interests her most is people and how they relate to their natural and unnatural environment. The unnatural environment is the one created by man: politics, economics, social hierarchies, inequalities. These issues are addressed, but subtly. They appear in her poems about the countryside and the implied social inequities therein, in her observations of severe environmental degradation, in her metaphors of wounds and bones, in her abandoned fields and defiled mountains.

Clearly there is considerable darkness to be found in Wang Xiaoni's poems, but that is far from her only mode.

> A gray overcast fair
> a half-day panting sluggish fair.
> Two motorcycles are filling up their tanks
> a pig is trussed up in the middle of the street
> the knife-sharpener wipes sweat from his nose.
>
> Who'd have thought the pig would escape in a blink
> shiny and black, it fled fast.
>
> It's fine to lose some things, but not the pig.
> The knife-grabbers, the bicycle-riders, the ones carrying scales
> the whole village gave chase,
> a streetful of black-clad galloping animals.
> —"At the Village Fair"

Here the pigs become like people and the people become pigs, those "black-clad galloping animals." Of course, as always in Wang Xiaoni's work, there is a deeper seriousness underpinning this poem. The final stanza reads: "And so the fair became a utopia / thanks to the one who declared war, thanks to those who didn't submit." In a country where speech and action are still closely regulated, submission is an issue faced every day, especially for a writer or artist.

Wang Xiaoni does not shy away from such issues, nor does she exploit them. Take for example the topic of religion, which is still sensitive territory. "The One Holding Peanuts" describes a scene that might bring to mind a Dorothea Lange photograph. There are naked children and an old woman, obviously living in poverty. The village water source has been polluted and "jumps with black bubbles." Yet the woman in the poem is "solid as a tall house." Why? "People say, this woman is religious." It's an understated poem and an understated last line that nevertheless recasts the whole piece. There is also a much larger sociological phenomenon at work here, that of the Chinese populous turning to religion of all kinds to offer meaning, or guidance, or community. This sense of searching, of a deep lack of moral compass, is pervasive in contemporary Chinese society. Wang uses a fine brush to capture the detail of the outer layers of scenes with such precision that the reader can readily fill in the gaps for him or herself.

Because her language tends toward the vernacular, Wang Xiaoni's poetry can seem deceptively simple to translate. One finds, however, returning to the original months or even years later, that there are resonances that have been muted or richer meanings that haven't come through in the translation. Wang's touch is light—she is an embroiderer who works with the finest thread to create careful tableaux. Each character, whether it is a shelf of coral, a lotus pond, or a graveyard guard, takes on its own luminescent life in the midst of the larger scene. Wang's tone is often leavened by an understated humor that counteracts her intense social conscience. This is not an easy balance, but Wang's musicality and precision of vision are guides. She is a self-protective poet: there are almost no love poems, scant details of her private life, very few elegies for loved ones. Or one might say that her gaze is directed outward.

This attention to the political and social realms is one of the challenges of translating Wang Xiaoni, and the reader should keep in mind the historical context as well. The poems here are presented in chronological order, beginning with work from the early 1980s and ending with a poem written in 2011. This shows Wang's development as a poet, and also gives the reader a rough timeline to follow. It helps to understand, for example, when reading (or translating) the 1980 poem "I Feel the Sun," that that year was the beginning of a decade of openness and hope, especially in literary and intellectual circles, and that at that moment Wang Xiaoni was a young college sophomore in the midst of it. "At last, I rush down the stairs, / pull open the door, / dash about in the spring sunlight. . . ." It also helps to know that after Mao Zedong was painted as "the red sun in our hearts," the sun as an image and as a rhetorical trope had to be recouped from its heavy political overtones. Wang was one of the poets able to reclaim language back from its misuse, and this is one of the reasons she became a leading figure at such a young age. Her ability to refashion language as a tool for art rather than propaganda, and her talent at creating startling and energized metaphors in a time of clichés serving political goals, makes her a vitally important writer still today.

Eleanor Goodman
Beijing, April 2014

SOMETHING CROSSES MY MIND

我感到了阳光

沿着长长的走廊
我，走下去……

——呵，迎面是刺眼的窗子，
两边是反光的墙壁。
阳光，我，
我和阳光站在一起。

——呵，阳光原来这样强烈！
暖得人凝住了脚步，
亮得人憋住了呼吸。
全宇宙的光都在这里集聚。

——我不知道还有什么存在。
只有我，靠着阳光，
站了十秒钟。
十秒，有时会长于
一个世纪的四分之一！

终于，我冲下楼梯，
推开门，
奔走在春天的阳光里……

I Feel the Sun

Down a long, long corridor
I keep walking . . .

—A window straight ahead so bright it hurts the eyes,
reflective walls on both sides.
Sunlight, me,
I stand with the sunlight.

—The sunlight is so intense!
So warm people stop in their tracks,
so bright people hold in their breath.
All the light in the universe collects here.

—I don't know that anything else exists.
There is only me, leaning on the sunlight,
stopping for ten seconds.
Ten seconds can be as long
as a quarter century!

At last, I rush down the stairs,
pull open the door,
dash about in the spring sunlight . . .

爱情

那个冷秋天呵

你的手
不能浸在冷水里
你的外衣
要夜夜由我来熨
我织也织不成的
那一件白又厚的毛衣
奇迹般地赶出来
到了非它不穿的时刻!

那个冷秋天呵
你要衣冠楚楚地做人

谈笑
我们一天天走过来
谈笑,使好人和坏人
同时不知所措
迎着眼睛
我拖着你的手
插进每一个
有良心的缝隙

我本是该生巨翅的鸟
此刻
却必须收拢翅膀
变一只巢
让那些不肯抬头的人
都看见
让他们看见

Love

Ah that cold autumn

Your hands
couldn't soak in cold water
your jacket
had to be ironed night after night
and that thick white sweater
I knitted and knitted in vain
was finished like a miracle
into a time when you'd wear nothing else!

Ah that cold autumn
you wanted to dress like a gentleman.

Talking and laughing
we passed the days
laughing and talking, we mystified
people both friendly and mean
in front of those eyes
I held your hand
and thrust myself into every
crevice with a conscience

I should have been born a giant bird
but now
I must draw in my wings
and become a nest
let all those unready to lift their heads
see me
let them see

天空的沉重
让他们经历
心灵的萎缩!

那冷得动人的秋天呵
那坚毅又严酷的
我与你之爱情

the heaviness of the sky
let them undergo
a withering of the soul!

Ah that autumn so cold it was poignant
that unyielding and bitter
love we had

那样想，然后这样想

首要的是你不在。
首要的是没有人在。
家变得广阔
睡衣凤凰般华贵。

我像皇帝那样走来走去。

灯光在屋顶
叫得很响。
我是它高高在上的回声。
一百六十四天
没人打开我的门。
我自然而然地做了皇帝。

穿上睡衣
日日夜夜地走。
我说话
没有什么不停下来倾听。

灰尘累累衣袖变厚。
平凡的人
从来没有见过
这么多会走会动的尘土。
从市上买回来的东西
低垂下手
全部听凭于我这个
灰尘之帝。

Thinking That, Then Thinking This

First and foremost, you're not here.
First and foremost, no one's here.
The house has become vast
pajamas as sumptuous as phoenix embroidery.

Like an emperor, I pace back and forth.

The ceiling lamp
calls loudly.
I am its echo from on high.
For one hundred and sixty-four days
no one has opened my door.
Naturally I have become an emperor.

Wearing pajamas
pacing night and day.
I speak,
and everything stops to listen attentively.

Dust spreads everywhere and my sleeves grow thick.
Ordinary people
have never seen
so much dust that can walk and move about.
Things bought at the market
droop from my hands
all of them listen to me
this emperor of dust.

报纸告诉我
外面永远是下雪的日子。
你再不能
二十岁般跳进来。
一百六十四天
你到人群中去挤。
变得比我还不伟大。
我干脆不想伟大。
这个世界无法清点所有房子
没人能寻找到我。

你不要回来
不要给我形容外面。
东方帝王
不必看世界
你让你的皇帝安息吧。

The newspaper tells me
it's always snowing outside.
You can't
jump in again like a twenty-year-old.
For a hundred and sixty-four days
you've been gone, out jostling through the crowds.
Becoming even less important than me.
I simply don't want to be important.
This world can't keep track of every house
no one can seek me out.

You don't want to come back
don't want to describe the outside world to me.
The monarch of the east
doesn't need to see the world
why not let your emperor rest.

不认识的人就不想再认识了

到今天还不认识的人
就远远地敬着他。
三十年中
我的朋友和敌人都足够了。

行人一缕缕地经过
揣着简单明白的感情。
向东向西
他们都是无辜。
我要留出我的今后。
以我的方式
专心地去爱他们。

谁也不注视我。
行人不会看一眼我的表情
望着四面八方。
他们生来
就不是单独的一个

注定向东向西地走。

一个人掏出自己的心
扔进人群
实在太真实太幼稚。

从今以后
崇高的容器都空着。
比如我
比如我荡来荡去的
后一半生命。

Those I Don't Know I Don't Want to Know

People I haven't already met
I'll respect from a distance.
Thirty years worth
of friends and enemies is enough.

Pedestrians pass by all the time
bearing uncomplicated emotions.
Heading east and west
they're all innocent.
I want to set aside my future,
and in my own way
focus on loving them.

No one watches me.
The pedestrians don't glance at my expression
as I look out in all directions.
They weren't born
the only one

doomed to wander all over.

Someone pulls out his heart
and throws it into the crowd
it's really too authentic too childish.

From today on
all the lofty vessels are empty.
For example me
for example this shiftless
last half of my life.

清晨

那些整夜
蜷曲在旧草席上的人们
凭借什么悟性
睁开了两只泥沼一样的眼睛。

睡的味儿还缩在屋角。
靠哪个部件的力气
他们直立起来
准确无误地
拿到了食物和水。

需要多么大的智慧
他们在昨天的裤子里
取出与他有关的一串钥匙。
需要什么样的连贯力
他们上路出门
每一个交叉路口
都不能使他们迷失。

我坐在理性的清晨。
我看见在我以外
是人的河水。
没有一个人向我问路
虽然我从没遇到
大过拇指甲的智慧。

金属的质地显然太软。
是什么念头支撑了他们
头也不回地
走进太阳那伤人的灰尘。

Early Morning

Those long nights
the people curled up on old straw mats
what insight do they rely on
to open their marshy eyes.

The smell of sleep still shrinks in the corners of the room.
Which part of their strength do they depend on
to stand up
carefully and precisely
to get food and water.

How much wisdom does it take
for them to take their keys
from yesterday's pants.
What force of connection is needed
when they set out on their journey
so that not a single intersection
makes them lose their way.

I sit in a rational dawn.
I see a river of people
beyond myself.
Not one asks me for directions
though I've never encountered
wisdom any greater than a thumbnail.

Metal is clearly too soft.
What thoughts sustain them
as they walk without turning back
into that dust as wounding as the sun.

灾害和幸运
都悬在那最细的线上。
太阳，像胆囊
升起来了。

Disaster and luck
both hang from the thinnest thread.
The sun, like a gallbladder,
rises.

看到土豆

看到一筐土豆
心里跟撞上鬼魂一样高兴。
高兴成了一个
头脑发热的东北人。

我要紧盯着它们的五官
把发生过的事情找出来。

偏偏是
那种昂贵的感情
迎面拦截我。
偏偏是那种不敢深看的光
一层层降临。

我身上严密的缝线都断了。

想马上停下来
把我自己整个停下来。
向烟瘾大的人要一支烟
要他最后的一支烟。

没有什么打击
能超过一筐土豆的打击。

回到过去
等于凭双脚漂流到木星。
可是今天
我偏偏会见了土豆。
我一下子踩到了
木星着了火的光环。

Seeing Potatoes

Seeing a basket of potatoes
I was as thrilled as if I'd encountered a ghost.
So thrilled I became
a feverish northeasterner.

I wanted to stare into their eyes
to find out all they'd been through.

Unexpectedly
unreasonable emotion
attacked me head-on.
A timid superficial light
fell layer upon layer.

All the precise sutures in my body broke.

I wanted to stop right away
stop myself completely
and bum a cigarette off an addict
his last cigarette.

Nothing can attack you
like a basket of potatoes.

Returning to the past
is like walking all the way to Jupiter.
But today
I saw a basket of potatoes.
All at once I was stepping
on Jupiter's burning rings.

一块布的背叛

我没有想到
把玻璃擦净以后
全世界立刻渗透进来。
最后的遮挡跟着水走了
连树叶也为今后的窥视
纹浓了眉线。

我完全没有想到
只是两个小时和一块布
劳动，居然也能犯下大错。

什么东西都精通背叛。
这最古老的手艺
轻易地通过了一块柔软的脏布。
现在我被困在它的暴露之中。

别人最大的自由
是看的自由。
在这个复杂又明媚的春天
立体主义走下画布。
每一个人都获得了剖开障碍的神力
我的日子正被一层层看穿。

躲在家的最深处
却袒露在四壁以外的人
我只是裸露无遗的物体。
一张横竖交错的桃木椅子
我藏在木条之内
心思走动。
世上应该突然大降尘土

A Rag's Betrayal

I hadn't expected
after I wiped the glass clean
the entire world would immediately infiltrate in.
The last shelter disappeared with the water
even the leaves thickened their eyebrows
to spy in.

I hadn't thought
such a mistake could be made
with only two hours of work and a rag.

Every thing is a master of betrayal.
This most ancient craftsmanship
was easily accomplished by a soft dirty rag.
Now I'm stranded in the midst of its exposure.

Other people's greatest freedom
is the freedom to see.
In this complex and beautiful springtime
cubism walks across the canvas.
Everyone has a superhuman power to traverse barriers
my life is penetrated in layers.

Hiding in the depths of the house
but exposed to people beyond these four walls
I'm just a poor bare body.
A thatched peachwood chair
I hide in its wooden strips
my thoughts restless.
The earth should be reduced to dust.

我宁愿退回到
那桃木的种子之核。

只有人才要隐秘
除了人
现在我什么都想冒充。

I'd rather return
to the pit of that peach tree seed.

Only humans want secrecy
now I'd like to pass myself off
as anything but human.

重新做一个诗人

在一个世纪最短的末尾
大地弹跳着
人类忙得像树间的猴子。

而我的两只手
闲置在中国的空中。
桌面和风
都是质地纯白的好纸。
我让我的意义
只发生在我的家里。

淘洗白米的时候
米浆像奶滴在我的纸上。
瓜类为新生出手指
而惊叫。
窗外，阳光带着刀伤
天堂走满冷雪。

每天从早到晚
紧闭家门。
把太阳悬在我需要的角度
有人说，这城里
住了一个不工作的人。

关紧四壁
世界在两小片玻璃之间自燃。
沉默的蝴蝶四处翻飞
万物在不知不觉中泄露。
我预知四周最微小的风吹草动
不用眼睛。

Starting Anew as a Poet

At the shortest end of the century
the earth bounces
humans busy themselves like monkeys between trees.

But my two hands
lie idle in China's air.
The tabletop and the wind
are both pure white paper.
I let my significance
happen only at home.

Rinsing white rice
the rice starch drips like milk onto my page.
To be reborn the gourds extend their fingers
and cry out in fear.
Outside, the sunlight cuts with a knife
heaven's cold heavy snow.

Each day from morning to night
the door is shut tight.
I hang the sun at the angle I need it
some people say, in this town
lives a person who doesn't work.

Fastened to the walls
between two small pieces of glass the world self-combusts.
The taciturn butterflies flutter everywhere
the universe unknowingly leaks its secrets.
I foretell the tiniest signs of trouble
without eyes.

不用手。
不用耳朵。

每天只写几个字
像刀
划开桔子细密喷涌的汁水。
让一层层蓝光
进入从未描述的世界。

没人看见我
一缕缕细密如丝的光。
我在这城里
无声地做着一个诗人。

Without hands.
Without ears.

Each day I write only a few words
like a knife
cutting into the gush of a tangerine's finely woven juice.
Let layer upon layer of blue light
enter into a world that's never been described.

No one sees my light
finely woven strand by strand like silk.
In this city I
silently serve as a poet.

月光白得很

月亮在深夜照出了一切的骨头。

我呼进了青白的气息。
人间的琐碎皮毛
变成下坠的萤火虫。
城市是一具死去的骨架。

没有哪个生命
配得上这样纯的夜色。
打开窗帘
天地正在眼前交接白银
月光使我忘记我是一个人。

生命的最后一幕
在一片素色里静静地彩排。
月光来到地板上
我的两只脚已经预先白了。

Moonlight Is Very White

Late at night the moon exposes every bone.

I breathe in a pale breath.
The world's irritations
become falling fireflies.
The city is a lifeless skeleton.

No life
can match this pure night light.
Open the curtains
and before my eyes the universe mixes with silver
the moonlight helps me forget I'm alone.

Life's last act
is silently rehearsed on a swath of white.
Moonlight arrives on the floorboards
my two feet are already pale.

从北京一直沉默到广州

总要有一个人保持清醒。
总要有人了解
火车怎么样才肯从北京跑到广州。

这么远的路程
足够穿越五个小国
惊醒五座花园里发呆的总督。
但是中国的火车
像个闷着头钻进玉米地的农民。

这么远的路程
书生骑在驴背上
读破多少卷凄凉的诗书。
火车顶着金黄的铜铁
停一站叹一声。

有人沿着铁路白花花出殡
空荡的荷塘坐收纸钱。
更多的人快乐地追着汽笛进城。

在中国的火车上
我什么也不说
人到了北京西就听见广州的芭蕉
扑扑落叶。
车近广州东
信号灯已经裹着丧衣沉入海底。

我乘坐着另外的滚滚力量
一年一年南北穿越
火车不可能靠火焰推进。

Silent All the Way from Beijing to Guangzhou

There must be someone who stays awake.
There must be someone who understands
only then will the train agree to run from Beijing to Guangzhou.

Such a long journey
enough to cut across five small countries
to startle awake five governors dozing in their gardens.
But a Chinese train
is like a peasant burrowing his way through a cornfield.

Such a long journey
a scholar riding on the back of a donkey
could read many dreary volumes of the classics.
The golden copper along the top of the train
sighs at every stop.

Along the tracks people hold bright white funerals
a deserted lotus pond turns a profit on paper money.
More people gladly chase the whistle into town.

On Chinese trains
I don't say a thing
at Beijing West people hear the Guangzhou banana trees
shaking off their leaves.
As the train nears Guangzhou East
the signals have sunk to the seafloor wrapped in mourning clothes.

I am riding some other rolling power
year after year crossing north and south
trains can't advance just on fire.

出门种葵花

春天就这样像逃兵溜过去了
路人都还穿着去年的囚衣。
太阳千辛万苦
照不绿全城。

一条水养着黄脸的平原
养着他种了田又作战
作了战再种田。
前后千里
不见松不见柳不见荷不见竹。

我不相信
那个荷兰人
会把金黄的油彩全部用尽。
我们在起风的傍晚出门
给灰沉的河岸
加一点活着的颜色。

种子在布袋里着急。
我走到哪儿
哪儿就松软如初。
肥沃啊
多少君王在脚下
睡烂了一层层锦绣龙袍。

在古洛阳和古开封之间
我们翻开疆土
给世人种一片自由的葵花看看。

Going Out to Plant Sunflowers

Spring sneaks past like an army deserter
pedestrians still wear last year's prison garb.
The sun with its many hardships
can't shine the whole city green.

A water-fed yellow-faced plain
feeds him, tills the fields, and does battle
after battle it goes back to tilling
a huge expanse
with no pines no willows no lotus no bamboo.

I don't believe
some Dutchman
will use up all the yellow paint.
We go out at nightfall as the wind rises
to give the heavy gray riverbank
a bit of vivid color.

The seeds are anxious in the bag.
Wherever I walk
is just as soft as before.
So fertile
and how many monarchs
have sullied their sumptuous many-layered robes underfoot.

Between ancient Luoyang and ancient Kaifeng
we open new territory
and plant sunflowers of freedom for the people to see.

蝉叫

蝉强迫我在粗砂纸间走
让我来来回回地难过。
又干又涩又漫长
十米以外爆炸开花的泡桐树
隐蔽很好的蝉在高处切我。

总有不怀好意的家伙
总有藏刀子的人。
今天轮到蝉了。

谁会去区别蝉和蝇和蜂
昆虫们都有荧荧发绿的内心。
从没正面端详过一个敌人
我始终被层层蒙蔽
一直到戏落而幕布缠身。
悲剧和喜剧都把力气用尽。
一点也不雪白
一点也不火红
一直到我不知不觉把颜色褪没了。

现在我走向隐蔽了蝉的泡桐
它像胆小鬼一样束立
天下肃静。

Cicada Call

The cicadas have me walking between sandpaper
they make it hard to come and go.
Dry and astringent and endless
the paulownia tree ten meters away explodes into bloom
cicadas loom well-hidden overhead.

There will always be bad guys
always people concealing knives.
Today it is the cicadas' turn.

Who can tell the difference between cicadas and flies and bees
all insects have green glimmering hearts.
I've never sized up an enemy face-to-face
so I'll be hoodwinked again and again
until the curtain falls and entangles me.
Tragedies and comedies have used up their strength.
Not snowy white
not fiery red
until I unconsciously shed all color.

Now I'm walking toward the paulownia that hides the cicadas
like a coward it just stands there
and the world is peaceful and still.

西瓜的悲哀

付了钱以后
这只西瓜像蒙了眼的囚徒跟上我。

上汽车啊
一生没换过外衣的家伙
不长骨头却有太多血的家伙
被无数的手拍到砰砰成熟的家伙。

我在中途改变了方向
总有事情不让我们回家。
生命被迫延长的西瓜
在车厢里难过地左右碰壁。
想死想活一样难
夜灯照亮了收档的刀铺。
西瓜跟上我
只能越走越远
我要用所有的手稳住它
充血的大头。

我无缘无故带着一只瓜赶路
事情无缘无故带着我走。

The Watermelon's Sorrow

After I've paid
the watermelon comes along like a blindfolded prisoner.

We get on the bus
this guy who's never changed his coat in his life
with no bones but too much blood
who grew up being thumped countless times.

Halfway there I take a turn
there's always something to keep us from home.
The watermelon with its artificially extended life
hits painfully off the sides of the bus.
It's as hard to want to die as it is to want to live
nightlights illuminate a closing knife shop.
The watermelon comes with me
it can only go farther and farther away
I'll use all my hands to steady its
big blood-filled head.

Without rhyme or reason, I carry the melon along
and without rhyme or reason, my busyness carries me.

徐敬亚睡了

在台风登陆前
徐敬亚这家伙睡着了。

现在徐变得比一匹布还安静
比一个少年还单纯。
那条睡成了人形的布袋
看起来装不了什么东西。

狂风四起的下午
棕榈拔着长发发怒
我到处奔跑关窗关门
天总是不情愿彻底垂下来。
徐真的睡了
疯子们湿淋淋撞门
找不到和他较力的对手。

一张普通木板
就轻松地托举起一个人。
我隔着雨看他在房中稳稳地腾云。

如果他一直睡着
南海上就不生成台风了。
如果他一直不睡
这世上的人该多么累。

最难弄的是人这件东西。

Xu Jingya Sleeps

Before the typhoon hits land
Xu Jingya sleeps.

Now Xu has turned quieter than a bolt of cloth
more innocent than a preteen.
The cloth bag shaped like a body from his sleep
doesn't look like it could hold a thing.

In an afternoon of wild wind rising everywhere
the palm trees pulled their long hair in anger
I ran around closing windows closing doors
the sky is never willing to collapse completely.
Xu actually slept
the lunatics were soaked and ran into doors
not finding an opponent of equal strength.

An ordinary plank
calmly lifted a man in its palm.
Through the rain I saw him in his house steadily riding the clouds.

If he'd kept sleeping
the South China Sea wouldn't have produced a typhoon.
If he hadn't slept at all
everyone in the world would have been exhausted.

The hardest thing to deal with is this thing called man.

在夜航飞机上看见海

什么都变小了
只有海把黑夜的皮衣
越铺越开。

向北飞行
右下方见到天津
左下方见到北京
左右俯看两团飞蛾扑着火。

这时候东海突然动了
风带起不能再碎的银片
又密又多的皱纹抽起来。

我看见了海的脸
我看见苍老的海岸
哆哆嗦嗦把人间抱得太紧了。

我见过死去
没见过死了的又这样活过来。

Seeing the Ocean from a Night Flight

Everything becomes small
only the ocean makes the night's leather clothes
open up the further out it spreads.

Flying north
to the right is Tianjin
to the left is Beijing
two clusters of moths flinging themselves at fire.

Then the East China Sea suddenly moves
the wind brings silver bits that can't be more shattered
and many thick wrinkles whip up

I see the face of the ocean
I see the aged seashore
trembling and hugging the world too tightly.

I have seen death
but never seen death come back to life like that.

11月里的割稻人

从广西到江西
总是遇见躬在地里的割稻人。

一个省又一个省
草木黄了
一个省又一个省
这个国家原来舍得用金子来铺地。

可是有人永远在黄昏
像一些弯着的黑钉子。
谁来欣赏这古老的魔术
割稻人正把一粒金子变成一颗白米。

不要像我坐着车赶路
好像有什么急事
一天跨过三个省份
偶尔感觉到大地上还点缀了几个割稻人。

要喊他们站起来
看看那些含金量最低的脸
看看他们流出什么颜色的汗。

November's Rice-Gleaners

From Guangxi to Jiangxi
I glimpse rice-gleaners bent to the ground.

In province after province
the vegetation yellows
in province after province
this country was once willing to pave the ground with gold.

Still there are always people at dusk
looking like bent black nails.
Who will come to admire the ancient sorcery
of rice-gleaners turning a bit of gold into a grain of rice.

Don't be like me hurrying along on the train
as though there's urgent business
crossing three provinces in a single day
occasionally noting the earth is still adorned with rice-gleaners.

I want to call for them to stand up
to see the faces worth the least gold
to see the color of sweat they produce.

喝点什么呢

酒太糙果汁太妩媚
水又太薄了。

合适的液体来不及生成。
树还没选中叶子
温泉没开窍
什么样的流动
能够配得上我现在这种绝妙的感觉。

没有一种为瞬间而生的液体。

时间就是短的。
十分钟以后
我可能什么也不需要了。
院子里的桂树偷偷开碎花
凤凰叹气落叶
穿毛外套的人原地散步。

飘飘的人尝不到飘飘的水
我很快
就将变回一个平凡了。

What Will You Have to Drink

Liquor is too harsh juice too cloying
water is too thin.

There isn't time to produce a suitable liquid.
The trees haven't yet settled on leaves
the hot springs haven't developed
and what flow
could match this cleverness I feel.

Nothing liquid can be born in an instant.

Time is short.
After ten minutes
I might not need anything.
The laurel trees in the courtyard bloom stealthily
the phoenix sighs fallen leaves
people in sweaters walk in place.

Self-satisfied people can't taste the flavor of water
I quickly
turn back into somebody ordinary.

耕田的人

那个人正扶着犁翻起整座山头。

他跟在牛的后面
他们两个正用力揭开土地的前额。
暗红的伤口露出来
能看见燃烧过后的红。
刑罚过后的红。
把疼痛默默挨过去的红。

矮小的耕田人忽然不见了
刚翻出来的红泥把他埋下山坡。
他的伙伴直挺起很大的头
好像另一个耕田人戴上了牛的面具
好像犁的前后两个亲兄弟。

烟草的种子还在麻布袋子里
劳动刚刚开始。
他们停下来
一高一低地咳嗽
后来，尘土蒙住脸，四周又静了。

Plowman

He is turning over the whole mountaintop with a plow.

He follows behind an ox
and the two reveal the earth's forehead by force.
A dark red wound appears
the red seen after a fever passes.
The red that comes after punishment.
The red that comes after pain has been quietly survived.

Suddenly the small plowman disappears
the just-turned red mud has buried him in the mountainside.
His partner raises his enormous head
like he's another plowman wearing an ox mask
like the pair at the front and back of the plow are brothers.

The tobacco seeds are still in the burlap sack
the work has just begun.
They stop
one coughing high the other low
then dust covers their faces, and everything is quiet again.

有了信仰的羊

羊群向着高处逃亡
皮毛很脏，心情很急。
前面的摔倒了后面的踩上来。
山坡越滚越快
还没融化的山顶已经很近了。

最后的几片雪出奇地白
天蓝得吓人
只有藏在深山里的羊才这样不顾一切
它们要去天上洗澡
干干净净地成仙。

山梁上起着风
追赶着，清洁着，神圣着这群小动物。
大团的白云和黑云都避开了
天留出最大的空间。

羊对羊群说话
导火索对火药说话
绝不让牧羊人靠近，不让他追上来。

要多么快才能甩掉牧羊人
把他塞回他的臭皮袍
把鼓在口袋里的三个馍塞进他的肚子。
把他留在他那个发臭的人间。

Religious Sheep

A flock of sheep flees up toward the peaks
with dirty coats, frightened.
Those in front who fall are stepped on by those behind.
The slopes roll faster and faster
and the not-yet thawed mountaintop is close.

The last few swaths of snow are extremely white
the sky so blue it's scary
only sheep hiding deep in the mountains would be this reckless
they want to go wash in the sky
cleanly and tidily becoming immortals.

The mountain ridges raise wind
to chase, to clean, to sanctify this group of small animals.
The mass of white clouds and black clouds avoid
the largest open space set aside by the sky.

A sheep speaks to the flock
a fuse speaks to gunpowder
never let a shepherd get near, don't let him catch up.

You have to be very quick to evade the shepherd
take him and stuff him back into his smelly leather chaps
take the three buns bulging in his pocket and stuff them down his gullet.
Leave him to his fetid human world.

麦苗们

成片成片的麦苗在山坡上发抖
越向上颤得越厉害
山快把自己抖碎了。

春天正借着风
向更远处传播着恐高症。
好像天的心里藏着透明的凶器
好像危险就要垂直刺下来。

有一束光在行走
太阳准备让绿色更绿。
麦苗正在流出害怕的胆汁
山头一个接一个传递，亮起来了。

麦子一直一直铺进乌黑的镇子
蒸在火上的馒头裂开了。
吃饱了的人出了门
拖起一条翻滚的红土尾巴。
红尾巴人领袖一样散步到山尖上
天下胆小的好像只是麦子。

绿色的害怕和锄头有关。
和镰刀那道锋利的光刃有关。
和吃面粉的我们有关。

Wheat Seedlings

On the mountainside field after field of wheat seedlings shiver
the farther up the more they tremble
the mountain will soon shake itself apart.

Spring borrows the wind
to spread a fear of heights even farther.
It seems a transparent weapon is hidden in the heart of the sky
it seems danger wants to drop down and stab us.

There is a bundle of light walking about
the sun is preparing to make the green even greener.
The wheat seedlings ooze bile in fear
one by one the mountaintops connect, light up.

The wheat keeps spreading into the pitch-black towns
the bread steamed on the fire breaks open.
Those who have eaten their fill go outside
to turn up a roiling red clay tail.
The red tail's human leader also strolls up to the mountaintop
the only thing on earth that seems timid is the wheat.

The green color's fear is of the hoe.
It's of the piercing bright blade of the sickle.
And it's of us, the flour-eaters.

那个人摔倒了

老太婆穿着她最好的衣服
夹着比两个老太婆还要高的芝麻杆。
全河南最小的脚走上了田埂
那生了她，又嫁了她的村庄越来越近。

她被怀里的芝麻绊倒
忽然摔在自己家挺挺的桐树下。
活过两个世纪的老太婆
在树影的迷乱里鹅一样大笑。
整个村子都忍不住动了。

像游在乡村中的金鱼
老太婆扑腾着刚染过布的两只靛蓝的手。
扑累了，照照很透亮的一汪天。

她的屋里存着最细最韧的棉花
架着最结实的织布机。
满院子晒着暖暖的新玉米
想到这些，她要在门口多睡一会。

芝麻都熟了，这季节让人踏实。
乡村原本应该是好的
庄稼白猫桐树和人都该享受好的生活。

The Woman Who Fell

The old woman is wearing her best clothes
carrying two sesame stalks taller than two old women.
The smallest feet in Henan walk the field ridges
and the village of her birth and marriage comes closer and closer.

She trips on the sesame stalks in her arms
and suddenly falls under the unyielding paulownia tree in her yard.
A woman who has outlived two centuries
laughs loud as a goose in the befuddlement of the tree's shadow.
The whole village can't help but move.

Like goldfish swimming through the countryside
the old woman flaps her hands turned indigo from dying cloth.
Tired of flapping, they mirror the bright pool of the sky.

In her room is the finest and strongest cotton
the most solid loom.
All over the courtyard warm new corn dries in the sun
thinking of this, she wants to sleep awhile in the doorway.

The sesame plants are all ripe, this season makes people practical.
The village is a good one
the crops and white cats and paulownia trees and people all enjoy a good life.

提着落花生的

她站着，两手提着刚出土的落花生。
那些果实，还穿着新鲜粉红的内衣
像婴儿，像没开瓣的荷花。

身后，一块田的距离
光光的立着她的五个小孙子。
他们的屁股上不是裤子
是快要僵硬的黄泥。
三块田的距离以外
坐着她已经不能行走的小脚母亲。

没有一个人移动，乡村出奇地安静
不知道他们在等什么。

落花生看到了最初的人间
一个挖掘者，五个小光人
远方还有一个苍老的。
泥土还没完全落干净
花生有点伤心。

她站着，稳稳地像任何大地方的高房子
满园鲜花的房子
管风琴奏乐的房子。
乡村的水塘远远地跳着黑汽泡
她的心正向外亮着。

人说，那妇女是个信教的。

The One Holding Peanuts

She stands up, her hands full of just-dug peanuts.
They still wear fresh pink underwear
like infants, like lotus flowers with unopened petals.

Behind her, a field away
her five grandchildren stand naked.
It isn't pants covering their behinds
but quickly-hardening mud.
More than three fields away
her hobbled mother sits with bound feet.

No one moves, the countryside is strangely quiet
who knows what they're waiting for.

The first thing these peanuts see of the human world
is a digger, five naked children
and an old woman in the distance.
The mud hasn't been cleaned off yet
and the peanuts feel a bit hurt.

She stands up, solid as a tall house on the earth
a house with a big flower garden
a house full of pipe organ music.
Far away the village pond jumps with black bubbles
her heart shines outward.

People say, this woman is religious.

泥屋前举着灯的那个

这种晚上举着一盏灯多不容易。
风来了，他就不见了
风停止又现出来
护着那油灯飘摇出门的人。

十分小心地走，蹑蹑地转过了两条街。
这么深，这么没人的夜里
只看见他火炭一样紧凑的五官
一小团谦卑的脸由着黑暗，向前游动。

那片泥屋有什么可照
容不下一头毛驴的石街有什么可照
这个世间又有什么可照的。
他不管，他不听那些，只是走
也许是黄牛生了，也许是妇人生了？

黑洞洞的世界，只有一捻光
只有时断时续的谦卑。
忽然什么也看不见了
村庄里的坡路，一直向下，要下很久。

The One Lifting a Lamp in Front of the Mud Hut

Raising a lamp at night like this isn't easy.
The wind rises, he disappears
the wind stops and he appears again
this man who's come out, shielding his swaying oil lamp.

Walking very carefully, tiptoeing past two streets.
A night so deep, so solitary
all that can be seen is his face tense as live charcoal
a small modest face in the dark, moving forward.

What does that mud hut have to illuminate
what do the cobbled streets too narrow for a donkey have to illuminate
what does the whole world have to illuminate.
He doesn't care, he doesn't listen to that sort of thing, he just walks on
maybe a cow has given birth, or maybe a woman?

In this pitch-black world, there is only a little pinch of light
there is only intermittent modesty.
Suddenly nothing can be seen
the village's sloping streets, going straight downhill, going down a long time.

在墟市上

灰蒙蒙的墟市
半天喘一口气的慵懒墟市。
两辆摩托车在加油
有一只猪被捆在街心
磨刀人刚擦掉满鼻梁的汗。

谁会想到那猪一转眼逃跑了
油黑油黑的，逃得真快。

少了哪个都可以，但是少不得猪。
抄刀的，骑车的，拿着称杆的
全镇都在追逃
满街穿黑衫狂奔的动物们。

猪的逃跑是今天的高潮
扔下了永远跑不掉的老镇子。
石板路又露出圆润的接缝
乌的瓦一层连一层
天光也显亮了
窗前开裂的泥盆，仙人掌争着开紫花。

这个时候的墟市成了桃花源
感激宣战者，感激那些不屈从的。

At the Village Fair

A gray overcast fair
a half-day panting sluggish fair.
Two motorcycles are filling up their tanks
a pig is trussed up in the middle of the street
the knife-sharpener wipes sweat from his nose.

Who'd have thought the pig would escape in a blink
shiny and black, it fled fast.

It's fine to lose some things, but not the pig.
The knife-grabbers, the bicycle-riders, the ones carrying scales
the whole village gave chase,
a streetful of black-clad galloping animals.

The pig's escape was the high point of the day
as he ditched this inescapable old town.
The flagstone streets showed their smooth junctures
layer after layer of crow-colored tiles
the morning turned bright
outside in a cracked mud pot, cacti competed to bloom purple flowers.

And so the fair became a utopia
thanks to the one who declared war, thanks to those who didn't submit.

穿裙子的稻草人

在这个国家的茫茫田野里
有穿裙子的稻草人。
她是唯一的一个
在古夜郎国的水田里微微斜立着。

城市淑女屋里出来的这件连衣裙
每一个夏天她都度过15岁。
她能飘能旋转，有时候还能飞一飞。

农民说，哪儿舍得裤子给个草人穿。
农民又说，城里捐来的不是些个好东西嚏。
他们咒骂那块花围布
作个稻草人，还干巴巴的是个女的。

乡间里来了穿裙子的稻草人
麻雀们顾不得粮食了
日夜围绕，欣赏城市小姑娘的模样。
从此古夜郎国的稻米很安全
一天天颗粒饱满
收割就快了。

Scarecrow in a Dress

In this country's wide open fields
there was a scarecrow wearing a dress.
She was the only one
standing a bit askew in the paddies of the ancient kingdom of Yelang.

Her dress came from a maiden in town
and every summer she turned fifteen again.
She could float and spin, and sometimes she could fly a little.

The farmers said, who'd put a scarecrow in a dress?
And the farmers said, in this town people don't throw out such nice stuff.
They cursed that flowery fabric
it was a scarecrow, but also a dried-up girl.

With this scarecrow in a dress from the village
the sparrows couldn't take care of the grain
day and night they circled, enjoying that town-girl style.
From then on the rice paddies of Yelang were safe
day after day the grains ripened
and the harvest was quick.

苏东坡的后人

整个村子静极了
没有狗叫，没有娃娃跑，没有公鸡打鸣。

满是青苔的老屋，满是青苔的老井。
清晨里的第一个人从古代出来，渐渐的
又矮又无语又迟缓。

后面跟着养蜂的，挖草药的，半披着彩服舞狮的
把能出售的东西都摆上街。
望着通往村外的石拱桥。

米酒都封紧在木桶里。
卖酒人说他的祖上是苏东坡
那就是全村人的名字。

在长江之中放船漫游的苏老头
他望月亮的眼神
现在正直直望着外乡游客的钱袋。

河流浅得行不了船
他们乘坐什么交通工具到了今天
把村庄住成一条木乃伊。

Descendants of the Poet Su Dongpo

The whole village is very still
no dogs call, no children run about, no roosters crow.

An old moss-covered hut, an old moss-covered well.
At dawn the first person emerges from antiquity, gradually
short and speechless and sluggish.

Bee-keepers, herb-gatherers, lion-dancers draped in colorful
              clothes followed
and spread out every sellable thing on the street.
They gazed at the stone arch bridge leading out of the village.

The rice wine was sealed up in wooden vats.
The wine-seller said Su Dongpo was his ancestor
so every villager is called by that name.

Old Su who roamed the Yangtze by boat
looked up at the expression in the moon's eyes
which were looking straight down at the tourists' wallets.

The river was so low the boat couldn't move
what vehicle did they take to get to this day
turning the village into a mummy.

到海里洗水牛

牛群被赶下了海，一路走到翻白的水沫里去。

肮脏的牛把大海神圣的边缘染黄
就像小僧人来过，投下几个肮脏的烂蒲团。

伟大的东西猛然起身
海在涨潮。
牛只有害怕
它们都是真正的老实人。
水发出最大声的恐吓
要驱赶这些四只脚的怪物。

赶牛的人躬着，清洗他精瘦的两条腿杆。
然后，赶牛人对海说，你凶什么
这点泥能污了你
你那么大！

牛张开心事重重的清澈眼睛
它看见蓝色的田地，比黄色的田地还要大
它们跟着海的节奏嚎叫
害怕赶牛人要耕这一大片的苦水。

像几个没穿衣服的害羞的绅士
走上海岸的牛放心了。
可是，太平洋追过来
它真的很生气。

Washing Water Buffalo in the Ocean

The herd was driven into the ocean, and into the churning white froth.

The filthy oxen dyed the ocean's holy edge yellow
as though a monk had come by, dropping a few rotting meditation cushions.

Something mighty suddenly stood up
the ocean was rising.
The oxen were afraid
they're the really honest ones.
The water threatened in its loudest voice
wanting to drive away these four-footed monsters.

The oxherd leaned down, washing his wiry legs.
Then the oxherd said to the sea, what are you yelling about
how can this little bit of mud pollute you
you're enormous!

An ox opened his anxious limpid eyes
it saw the blue field, even bigger than a yellow field
they bellowed in the ocean's rhythm
afraid the oxherd wanted to plough the huge stretch of bitter water.

Like a few unclothed and bashful gentlemen
the oxen strolled along the shore.
But the Pacific overran them
totally furious.

过云南记

老虎退下去，鹰也退下去
杀人的和被杀的都逃到了外省。
天腾出它的左下角
云南就在那下面蒙头睡觉。

这个红色庄园主睡得太舒服了
横侧着的曲线忽然高忽然圆。
绿袍子以下露出红的身体
比红还深，比岩石还深
比种子的要求还深。

只有红，没有火
只有身体，没有主人。
青草们爬上它的头顶心惊肉跳
峡谷的牙齿闪着懒惰的光。

泥土被玉米根簇拥着发胖
红色的云南不做事也不慌张。
现在，左右奔跑着空山回声
我紧提着心经过一条铅红色的舌头。

Thoughts Upon Crossing Yunnan

The tigers retreat, the hawks retreat too
the killers and the killed flee to other provinces.
The sky clears its lower left corner
below Yunnan covers its head to sleep.

This red lord of the manor sleeps comfortably
from the side the curves are suddenly high and round.
A red body shows beneath the green robe
deeper than red, deeper than cliffs
deeper than the demands of seeds.

There is only red, not fire
there is only a body, not a lord.
The grass climbs up to the top of its head and shakes with fear
the canyon's teeth sparkle with lazy light.

The soil grows fat with clusters of corn
red Yunnan doesn't work and doesn't get flustered.
Now, empty mountain echoes run everywhere
I hold tight to my heart and pass through the red lead tongue.

过广西记

最透明的早上，玻璃的早上
世界从下到上都变成晃眼的黄色。

收割稻子的广西正走向山的最高处
夹着刀的那个小金人
站着比坐着还要矮的那个劳动者。
它说稻米长到了龙的脊梁上
龙的妹妹卷起舌头就唱一支歌
她让我看见幸福就是痛苦在打滚儿。

今年的粮食又压在黄牛的身上
可是，广西只顾讲述龙脊梁的故事。

晚上一点点黑下去沉下去
天没了，广西和它的龙也紧跟着没了。
只是竹榻上还睡着人
白天里吞了金的名叫广西的这个人
重重地倒下了。
金子的重量刚好是稻米的重量。

秋天，是黄金大削价的季节
我得了深层的恐高症。
广西在疲倦的九月之夜翻身
龙和它染了色的铠甲们雪一样落地
真实的月亮像鱼钩弹起来了。

Thoughts Upon Crossing Guangxi

Most transparent morning, a glass morning
from top to bottom the world turns dazzling yellow.

Rice-gleaning Guangxi is walking toward the mountains' highest peak
a little metal statue clutching a knife
a worker who's even shorter standing up than sitting down.
It says the paddies have grown onto the dragon's back
the dragon's little sister rolls her tongue and sings
she makes me see happiness is just pain rolling over.

This year's grain weighs down the oxen again
but Guangxi only tells the tale of the dragon's back.

Evening slowly darkens, slowly falls
day disappears, soon after Guangxi and its dragon disappear.
Still the bamboo beds hold sleeping men
and the one called Guangxi who during the day gulps down gold
collapses layer by layer.
Gold's weight equals the weight of rice.

Autumn is the season of discounted gold
I have developed a profound fear of heights.
Guangxi turns over on weary September's nights
the dragon and its dyed scales fall to the ground like snow
the true moon snaps out like a fishhook.

过贵州记

贵州半隐半露着。
从古到今最骨感的这个模特儿
它把身体深藏在骷髅遍布的山间。
左右的溶洞里挂满了它的时装
取一件是黑的，取一千件还是黑的。

骨瘦如枝的贵州胆小又紧张
越坐越古老越陷越深
像黑山羊的尸体钻出风暴掀乱的墓地。

太阳的光正调教大地上的花豹
那是它们两个之间的游戏
西边亮起来，东边又暗下去。
想像中的猛兽扑住无辜的山脊不放
贵州用力耸起全身的硬度
永远拿不到时刻表
它特圆的眼睛永远干瘪着不善于张望。

那人全身都是秘密
被埋藏的还活着，露出来的先死了。
碑石碎成一地的石匠的墓园
紧守着这世上最后一个没出场的守墓人。

Thoughts Upon Crossing Guizhou

Guizhou is half hidden, half revealed.
The boniest model in history
it hides its body deep in the skeleton-scattered mountains.
The limestone caves everywhere are hung with its trendy clothes
grab one and it will be black, grab a thousand and they'll all be black.

Twig-frail Guizhou is timid and nervous
the older the longer it sits there, dug in deeper and deeper
like a cemetery where a black goat's corpse has been unearthed in a windstorm.

The sunlight trains a mottled leopard on the earth
it's a game for the two of them
the west lightens, the east darkens.
An imaginary beast pounces on an innocent mountain ridge and won't let go
Guizhou strains to harden its whole body
unable to get on schedule
its round eyes are too shriveled to see clearly.

That person's whole body is secret
what has been buried still lives, what is revealed dies first.
Headstones are smashed into a stonemason's cemetery
beside the world's last off-stage graveyard guard.

荷塘鬼月色

荷塘是漆黑的。
冬天霸占了荷塘，存放这一年的尸体。
哪儿有半丝的月色。

12月里闲适的枯骸
演戏的小鬼们舞乱了月亮的水面。
焦炭还要再披件灰烬的袍子
干柴重新钻进火
寒冷的晚上又黑了10倍。
月色水一样退回天上的盘子。

那片魔沼里的蛙
偶尔滚一下冰凉的鹅卵石
有人想招回光亮，想刺破这塘死水。
可是鬼不答应，鬼们全在起身
荷花早都灭了
到处遗弃它们骨瘦如柴的家园。

迎面飘过一张忽然很白的脸
人的微光出现在深夜和凌晨之间。
那个沙沙沙过路的
不会是心情总不宁静的朱自清吧？

Lotus Pond Ghost Moonlight

The lotus pond is lacquer-black.
Winter occupies the pond, depositing this year's corpses.
And where are the half-threads of moonlight?

December's comfortable dry bones
little playacting ghosts dance the moon's watery surface wild.
Petroleum coke puts on another robe of ashes
firewood burrows into the fire again
the frigid evening darkens tenfold.
Moonlight like water returns to its dish in the sky.

The frogs in that eerie marsh
every so often turn over the icy pebbles
there are those who want to bring back the light, want to pierce
                this stagnant pool.
But the ghosts don't agree, they all rise up
the lotus flowers long ago perished
abandoning their bone-dry home.

Ahead floats a face turned suddenly white
man's faint light appears between the deep night and dawn.
That one rustling past
could he be Zhu Ziqing, that ever-restless poet?

闪电之夜

闪电之夜让人着迷。

有些异象跟着雷来
跟着光来
很可能还跟着几只鬼。

我或有或无
一会儿消失，一会儿又出现。
谋杀的闪光里藏着飞快缝合的手。

人坐在黑暗中
消失的时间很长
出现只是一眨眼。

所有的黑衣人，所有的忍者。
没见匕首，没见受伤的
只有突然深的裂缝
突然出声的惨白。
天啊，伤口合拢得太快了
它不能被看清。
说谎的少年最快地闭紧没血色的嘴唇。

我知道，这会儿我还在。
可是我完全不知道
在我以外的全部。

Nights of Lightning

These nights of lightning fascinate.

Strange images follow the thunder
follow the light
and likely follow a few ghosts.

Perhaps I have or haven't
disappeared for a while, then after a while appeared again.
The rapidly suturing hand hides in the sparkle of the murderer.

People sit in the dark
disappearing takes a long time
appearing happens in the blink of an eye.

All the people wearing black, all those who endure.
Not seeing the dagger, not seeing the injured
there is only a sudden deep rift
the sudden sound of paleness.
Oh, the wound closes so quickly
it can't be seen.
The children telling lies are the quickest to close their bloodless lips.

I know, I'm here for now.
But I don't know anything
about what's outside of myself.

深夜的高楼大厦里都有什么

可以没有人，但是不能没有电。
电把梯子送上去
再把光亮送上去
把霓虹灯接到天上。

人们造好高楼大厦
人赶紧接通了电就撤退了。
让它独自一个站在最黑暗的前线
额头毒亮毒亮
像个壮丁，像个傻子
像个自封的当代英雄。
浑身配戴闪闪的奖章，浑身藏着炸药
浑身跑着不断向上的血。

而现在的我抖开烫过的床单
我灭了所有的灯。
高楼大厦们亮得不行
我吃了闭眼睛的药。
这一生能做一个人已经无限无限美好。

At Night What's Inside the Skyscrapers

There need not be people, but there can't not be electricity.
Electricity sends the steps up
and sends the light up
sends neon into the sky.

People built a skyscraper
they hurried to put in electricity and then withdrew.
Let it stand alone at the darkest battlefront
forehead poisonously bright
like an able-bodied man, like an idiot
like a self-proclaimed hero.
Its whole body covered in sparkling metals, its whole body hiding explosives
its whole body leaking blood toward the sky.

And now I expose the ironed sheets
I put out all the lights.
The skyscrapers are unbearably bright
I take an eye-closing pill.
In this life to be human is already glorious.

在冬天的下午遇到死神的使者

那个在银夹克里袖着手的信使。

我们隔着桌子对视
桌上满满的滚着红到了顶的脐橙。
光芒单独跳过来照耀我
门外的旅人蕉像压扁了的尸体
古典武士正受着刑罚。

那是个不能形容的忠诚的人
看样子就叫人信赖。
沉默在沉默后面赶紧说话
好像该草签一张有关未来的时间表。

可是，我现在还不能从我里面钻出去。
跑也不行
挣扎也不行
纵身一跳也不行。
我能做的最惊天动地的事情
就是懒散地坐在这个用不上力气的下午。
时间亏待了我
我也只能冷落他了。

月亮起身，要去敲响它的小锣
我打开了门，我和死神的信使左右拥别
拿黄昏最后一线光送他。

Meeting Death's Envoy on a Winter Afternoon

That messenger with his hands tucked in the sleeves of his silver jacket.

From across the table, we watch
red navel oranges roll all over the table.
The light leaps over to illuminate me
outside the palm trees look like flattened corpses
ancient warriors receiving their punishment.

He's nondescript, a faithful man
one who could be called trustworthy.
Behind silence's back silence speaks quickly
as though signing off on a timetable for the future.

I still can't tunnel out from my insides.
It's no good to run
no good to struggle
no good to leap away.
The most I can do to try to move heaven and earth
is to sit lazily in this listless afternoon.
Time has treated me badly
all I can do is shun him.

The moon rises, goes to ring its small gong
I open the door, and Death's messenger and I part ways
I use dusk's last light to send him off.

那个人，他退到黑影里去了

灯捏在手心里。
他退到煤粉熏暗了的巷子最深处
还退到黑色的灯芯绒中
退进九层套盒最紧闭的那一只
月亮藏住阴森的背面。
他一退再退
雪地戴上卖炭翁的帽子
那个人完全被黑暗吃透了。

而他举着的手电筒迟缓了那么半步
光芒依旧在。
在水和水纹中间
在树木正工作的绿色机芯里
在人们暗自心虚的平面
幽幽一过。

所有的，都亮了那么一下
游离了恍惚了幻象了
这种最短的分离，我一生只遇见过三次。

The Man Retreats into the Shadows

Holding a lamp in his palm.
He retreats deep into the alley in the coal dust's smoky dark
then retreats into the floss of the black wick
retreats into the tightest layer of a nine-layer box
the moon conceals its dismal back.
He retreats and retreats
the snow puts on the hat of an old charcoal seller
the man is completely eaten up by the dark.

But he raises a flashlight and slowly trudges on
the light is still there.
Between the water and the water ripples
in the trees' green working mechanisms
on people's inner level of shame
it passes faintly.

Everything shines at once
drifting, distracted, phantasmal
this briefest separation I've seen only three times in my life.

贴着白色墙壁走掉的人

他贴着他自己走。
他的灵魂紧随着，清楚地出现在稍后的墙上。

他一点都没察觉到分离
一点不看重那件破东西
他让那家伙独自一个。
灵魂遇到苍蝇，苍蝇也逃开
遇到墙上的涂鸦，肮脏的字蹦跳躲闪。

他只顾自己快步走，贴着苍白可怜的墙。
前面是他
后面是脚不落地的灵魂
歪歪扭扭跟得紧
好像很害怕迷失的痛苦
那个孤苦伶仃的弃儿。

如果人走得快一点
可能甩掉他那个心事重重的尾巴。
再快一点
那面墙就和路人无关
只是冬日里一整片的好阳光。

The One Sticking Close to the White Wall as He Leaves

He sticks close to himself as he leaves.
His soul follows close behind, appearing on the wall.

He doesn't notice the separation at all
doesn't care about that old thing
he leaves it all on its own.
The soul meets a fly, the fly escapes
it encounters graffiti on the wall, the filthy words leap and dodge.

Caring only for himself he hurries on, sticking to the wretched graying wall.
In front is himself
behind is the hovering soul
twisting and turning to follow close
as though terrified to lose its way
that poor helpless little orphan.

If he walks a little faster
he might lose that anxious tail.
Even faster
and the wall won't have anything to do with the passersby
just one large swath of good winter sunlight.

你找的那人不在

他根本不在。
其它的都在，只是你要的不在。

有东风进来
有小昆虫进来
星光像刚刚磨碎了的面粉。
西红柿成熟了的橙黄色进来。
海马从落地窗最低的缝隙间游进来。
陌生人经过，不知名的烟草香味透进来。

我这儿从来没这么满过。
什么都有，什么都不缺少
温暖友善的东西们四处落座。

我们不在同一个世界
四月是隔绝的屏风
所以，你只有原路退回
你找的人他绝不会在。

The One You're Looking for Isn't Here

He simply isn't there.
Everyone else is there, only the one you want isn't here.

An eastern wind comes in
small insects come in
the starlight is like just-milled flour.
The orange of tomatoes ripening comes in.
From the French window's lowest crack seahorses swim in.
Strangers pass by, the scent of cheap cigarettes floats in.

I've never had so much before.
Everything is there, nothing is lacking
warm friendly things sit all around me.

We're not in the same world
April is a dividing screen
you can only go back the way you came
and the one you're looking for won't ever be here.

月光之一

月亮意外地把它的光放下来。
温和的海岛亮出金属的外壳
土地显露了藏宝处。

试试落在肩上的这副铠甲
只有寒光，没有声响。
在银子的碎末里越走越飘
这一夜我总该做点儿什么。

凶相借机躲得更深了
伸手就接到光
软软的怎么看都不像匕首。

Moonlight, No. 1

The moon unexpectedly casts its light.
A warm ocean island's metal shell glints
and the earth shows its hidden treasures.

This armor that practices falling onto shoulders
gives off only a cold light, and no sound.
In silver fragments that float farther and farther
tonight I should at least find something to do.

Violence takes its chance to hide even deeper
an outstretched hand reaches the light
so soft that no matter the angle it never looks like a dagger.

月光之二

那个好久都不露面的皎白的星体
忽然洞穿了夜晚的一角。

天光下正交谈的路人
嘴里含满快滚落出来的珠子。
浮淡的光泽扑动着
嘤嘤的，好像是提着玉佩的唐朝。

我要一直留在家里
留在人间深暗的角落。
时光太厚，冬衣又太重了
飞一样，倒换着放帘子的手
遮挡那只当空的鹰眼。

Moonlight, No. 2

That bright-white long-absent star
suddenly pierces through a corner of the night.

Passersby chat in the daylight
their mouths full of dropping pearls.
A thin sheen flutters
whispering, like the jade-wearing Tang Dynasty.

I want to stay at home forever
stay in the world's dark corners.
Time is too thick, winter clothing too heavy.
Like flying, hands take turns closing the curtains
to keep out the sky's eagle eye.

月光之三

海正在上岸，盐啊，摊满了大地
风过去，一层微微的白
月光使人站不稳。

财富研出了均匀的粉末
天冷冷的，越退越远，又咸又涩。
那枚唯一升到高处的钱币就要坠落了
逃亡者遍地舞着白旗。

银子已经贬值，就像盐已经贬值。
我站在金钱时代的背面
看着这无声的戏怎么收场。

Moonlight, No. 3

The ocean is coming ashore, ah salt, spreading over the earth
the wind blows past, a layer of barely perceptible white
the moon makes people unsteady.

Wealth grinds equality to a powder
the sky is very cold, retreating further and further, salty and astringent.
The only coin that rose to the top is about to drop
all around fugitives brandish white flags.

Money has depreciated, like salt has depreciated.
I stand on the other side of this age of wealth
and watch how the silent drama will play out.

台风之一

台风之夜，天空满了，人间被扫荡。

从西向东，成群的黑牛在头顶上打滚
风的蹄子一遍一遍捣窗
地上的一切都要升天了。

人装在夜里
夜晚装在正爆开的鼓里。
狂妄的气流
从另外的世界推出滚滚战车。
没见到丝毫的抵抗
了不起的事情就是这样发生的。

Typhoon, No. 1

The night of the typhoon the sky was full, the world destroyed.

From west to east, herds of black cattle rolled on their heads
the wind's hoofs beat at the windows
everything on the ground rose to the sky.

The people were packed into the night
the night was packed into an exploding drum.
The wildly arrogant air
presented rolling tanks from another world.
There was no sign of resistance
that's just the way the extraordinary happens.

台风之二

植物割断了长发
遍地跳着来不及死去的神经
疯子撞破了疯人院
终于轮到疯子们庆贺胜利了。

我在鱼肚子里坐稳
满心的颠簸，满心跑着大云彩。

天堂拔出电的鞭子。
风雨压扁了城市
刮尽它最后那层浮光闪烁的金鳞。
得意的人转眼败下去
膨胀在窗前的荷塘一下子矮多了。

Typhoon, No. 2

The plants chopped off their long hair
nerves that hadn't had time to die jumped everywhere
madmen destroyed the madhouse
it was finally their turn to celebrate a victory.

I sat firmly in a fish-belly
heart jolting, heart running on the clouds.

Heaven pulled out an electric whip.
Wind and rain flattened the city
scraped off its last layer of glittery golden scales.
All the complacent people quickly retreated in defeat
the lotus pond swelling outside the window suddenly dropped.

害怕

1.

是没有先兆的，是一下子的
偶然翻开一些影像的间隙，最终的闸门爆破了

垮掉的水被天空放出来，漫过梳妆打扮的木棉树
从那个哑人废掉的嗓子，跑出四面漫开的大沙漠
玻璃的前后，其实正是荒原深处

滩涂奇怪地亮，像大鱼刚剥开腥气的皮
白色的扇面上，舞动着几个软骨头的动物
人类即将退场，报幕者最先死去，断臂堆积成小山

什么也不发生的空空朗朗的日子
一定有人大难当头了，危险试着深浅正摸索过来

接下来，海将要凝固成盐田，它要一点点褪回咸苦的本色
不可知的事物又要由海重新开始，秘密层层张开
我们在水晶的抛光面上摔倒，不能起身

良心越跑越快，逃跑的车刹不住了
没有安全地带，树上垂着缠绕中的麻绳，倒悬的菠萝蜜
不紧不松，不吃不喝，不哭不笑
还有，集体起身鼓掌的那一群，鬼出来指挥了
他们为什么整齐地拍手？拍自己的手，又像拍打着所有的别人？

Fear

1.

It comes without warning, all at once
tearing open cracks between images, breaking down the last sluice

Water collapses from the sky, flowing past the decked-out kapok trees
a desert overflows from a mute's abandoned throat
a deep wasteland on both sides of the glass

The shoals have a peculiar shine, like large fish stripped of reeking skins
on the white fans, a few soft-boned creatures dance
mankind soon exits, the stage manager dies first, broken arms pile up

On unreal days where nothing happens
people face devastation, danger fumbles past testing its depths

After, the ocean solidifies into a salt plain, it slips bit by bit back to its bitter
                    salt nature
unknowable creatures rise anew from the ocean, secretly opening in layers
while we slip on the crystals' polished surface, unable to stand

Conscience runs faster and faster, an escaping car without brakes
nowhere's safe, tangled hemp ropes are hung in trees, upside-down jackfruits
not tense or loose, not eating or drinking, not crying or laughing
and a ghost emerges to direct the collective that stands and applauds
why are they all clapping in time? Clapping their hands like they're slapping
                    each other?

2.

远离那唱歌的，他是怎么了，张开嘴就让声音跑出来
要格外躲避没有请到乐队的清唱
在没有听众的地方，唱着很快就会变成哭着

海滩上用黄沙反复掩埋自己的人
玩消失，玩自杀，掉进人间游戏的陷阱
那颗勉强暴露的头，是一颗由内向外腐烂的白菜

稻子刚收割过的下午，秸秆都还垛在田野里
那些断了命的沮丧的雄狮，满身披散仓惶的头发
从春到秋活着的只有稻草人，乡村早就消灭了理发师

柚木的桶，装了一半清水
水里有汽泡，有香草，有茉莉花瓣，有塑胶天使
这时候，猛然跳进一个亮似月光的肮脏泥人

跟在汽车后面疯跑的，吐出了机器的气息
有人清嗓儿，有人要领袖一样宣讲什么
他们说打开那盏灯那盏灯那盏灯，明晃晃的能说出什么

端起酒瓶的，带着阴谋的人
笑得前仰后合，嘴巴正对着阴天的人
满眼的走进来又走出去
不知道鞋是否有底，脚是否还连接腿杆

山又高了，水又深了，世界又乖巧地躬身懊悔了
什么时候花言巧语都呈送上来
每一个都别想有尊严地了结，每一个都不确信自己是一个人

咖啡刚煮好，灵魂是21克，速溶的一袋13克
摇晃那浅浅的小半杯，喝还是不喝

2.

What's wrong with that distant singer, his voice runs from his open mouth
hoping to avoid unaccompanied arias
in a place with no audience, singing quickly turns to crying

Those on the beach who bury themselves over and over in yellow sand
play at disappearing, play at suicide, fall into the trap of people's games
the head forced to expose itself is a cabbage rotting from the inside

The afternoon after the rice harvest, sorghum stalks remain piled in the fields
those dead disheartened lions, frazzled hair hanging from their bodies
scarecrows are the only living things from spring to autumn, the village long
                    ago abolished hairdressers

A teak bucket, half-filled with clear water,
bubbles in the water, and sweetgrass, jasmine petals, a plastic angel
and then, a filthy clay figure bright as moonlight leaps in

A smell leaks crazily from the back of cars, spat out from machines
someone clears his throat, someone wants to speechify like a leader
they say turn on that lamp, and those lamps, shining so something can be said

Those holding wine bottles and scheming
those shaking with laughter, those with mouths open to the overcast sky
get an eyeful going in and out
they don't know if their shoes have soles, if their feet and legs are still connected

The mountains rise again, the water deepens, the world sweetly bows in remorse
when will all the sweet-talk be sent up
no one expects a dignified end, no one is convinced of his own humanity

The coffee is ready, the soul is 21 grams, dissolved coffee packet 13 grams
tilting that light half glass, to drink or not to drink

3.

楼梯们，桥梁们，拱形隧道们，还有高速公路
四面八方，它们私下通敌已经很久
它知道，而人不知道，前方早被它们瓜分垄断了

那些垒得超级整齐的红砖，看起来挺不错
比红还红的固体终于也稳不住了
寓言给每个人提着钥匙，引诱你乖乖住进去

带话儿的人，他说的，一定不是他想的
旧的友善全都淡了，新的还不准备发生

穿戏装的人，在黑暗幕布后面赶紧列队
提词的人，举着台词像举着真理
陈年旧事团团旋转，画眉涂眼重新排练演出

男低音女低音，太闷了太堵了，太惊世骇俗了
高音是假声，中音是半个假声，世上没人听到过真声

钉得均匀的笼子，落地的，不落地的窗子
开始用铁造，后来用合金，现在改用不锈钢了
那些是专门用作装置我们的器皿和牢房

还有，把书页忽然照亮的，呆在床头的台灯
看看它照耀的结果，白纸更白，黑字更黑
比蛇还神秘的弯曲的物体，模仿了人类体温的密探
人读到了哪儿，那团叫作灯的光芒，紧跟着就去破译

雪到底落了下来，天地抖得不成个样子
那种白，可不敢深看
那是有内劲儿的，责难的，冷笑的，静观事变的

3.

Stairs, bridges, arched tunnels, and highways
far and wide, they've long collaborated with the enemy in secret
they know what man doesn't, they long ago partitioned and monopolized
        the front

These neatly stacked bricks seem pretty good
but in the end redder-than-red solids won't hold up either
fables bring each person a house key, and lure you to obediently move in

Talkative people, he said, are not the ones he misses
the old friendliness has faded, and the new isn't ready

The ones in costume quickly line up behind the dark curtain
the prompters hold up the actors' lines as though holding up the truth
old business revolves, putting on makeup and rehearsing again from the start

Bass and contralto, too stuffy and stopped up, all too astonishing
tenor is falsetto, alto half-falsetto, no one on earth has ever heard a real voice

The evenly-nailed cage falls to the ground, the window that doesn't fall
once used iron, then alloys, now stainless steel
all used specially for our household utensils and prisons

And the bedside reading lamp that suddenly lights up the page
look at the results of its illumination, white paper more white, black words
        more black
an object more mysteriously twisted than a snake, a spy imitating human warmth
whatever people read is decoded by that collection of rays called a lamp

Snow finally falls, the universe shivers out of shape
no one dares stare into that kind of white
with its inner energy, blame, sneers, quiet emergencies

4.

节日们，东方的春节元宵，还有西方的圣诞老红人
躲过哪一劫都不容易，可是没人退后，水仙预先香起来
放爆竹的，狂奔购物的，城市们的心乱透了

点灯的人忽然把光招进来
夜晚的天空变远，而他自己不敢近前，他怕晃坏眼睛

重庆巫山的群峰，腰间珍藏着小土豆
土豆上面是土，土豆下面是石头
满山圆头圆脑的孤儿，那就是我们最后的供养者

南方的树冠优雅地生孩子，不要以为又有弱小出世了
我们的骨头簌簌的电一样疼
电没带来一件好东西，它将在人类之前最先被鞭挞

春天夏天秋天冬天，分别装了四个轮子神转
四只胎铃就快跑成一堆零碎
那里面充满的不再是气体，是不受控制的筋腱
承重的柱子快倒了，从1层到28层，将被迫成为一家人

人们写过的字，实在没什么意思
我不想再承认它们，推倒了，也不要重新来
不经意里看到的全是伤心，惯性让人流眼泪
实在难以保住一个内心结实的人，一个也没有

半圆的球体，纯麻的织物，透明的瓷
不知道在我以后，还有谁继续爱惜依恋它们
我不愿意向前追究，但是，我能确定
它们每一件都被另一些战战抖抖的手小心制作
我还没结识过不害怕的人

4.

Holidays, the East's Spring Festival dumplings, and the West's Christmas Santa
it's hard to avoid such disasters, but no one retreats, the narcissus turns fragrant
the firecracker-lighting, crazily-shopping cities are thoroughly distracted

The man turning on the lamp suddenly invites in the light
the night sky turns distant, and he doesn't dare get close, fearing it will blind him

The peaks of Chongqing's Mt. Wu collect little potatoes at their waist
above the potatoes is soil, below the potatoes is stone
those round-headed orphans of round-tipped mountains are our last offering

Southern treetops give birth elegantly, but don't think their offspring weak
our bones ache like rustling electricity
electricity has brought no good, it will be punished before humans are

Spring summer fall winter, differentiated by four wheels that turn magically
four hubcaps quickly turn into a pile of junk
what fills them is no longer gas, but uncontrollable sinews
all the load-bearing pillars will soon collapse, and from the 1st to the 28th floor,
                    everyone will be forced to live together

The words people have written are meaningless
I don't want to acknowledge them anymore, they're gone and won't return
all that is carelessly read is hurtful, inertia leads to tears
there really is no one who can't keep a strong heart

Half-globes, hemp cloth, transparent porcelain
after I'm gone, who will continue to treasure them, to long for them
I don't want to find out, yet I can be sure
each one was carefully made by trembling hands
I've never known a person who wasn't afraid

最后得说到死，因为死掉以后什么都不再知道
最可怕的是死之前，没有商量没有缝隙，人是完全被蒙蔽的
看起来已经很多了，而害怕没有穷尽
从容窜过快速车道的小老鼠，它的胆子
比10个人类相加在一起还要大

5.

一直一直，我都清楚，我是个胆子极小的人
只会安心做点儿细微的没危险的事情

从没想过改变什么
特别是密密实实镶雕在头顶上的一道道真理
虽然它根本不配横在人前

已经很久很久了，使人受害和受益的都是洞穿力
从来没感到过安全，就像我抬头总看见黑云正经过着天

总以为胆小是一个人的心事
可是害怕终于现身了，它直接撞过来
不能解释的，近在三公分之内的硬物，那就是害怕
那正是它本人

一点点地靠拢，渺小的，不识字的，安祥的全裹藏其中
谁都在，谁也摘不掉，谁也逃不成
人除了害怕，什么也不能做

没有一个无辜者，就像没有人不害怕
谁也不放弃，谁也不饶恕，没有人应该得到保护
勇敢的解释早该推翻重来，人要醒悟，他只能被害怕压着
就像12月的北方，他必须盖紧厚棉絮造的被子

One finally must bring up death, because after death there is no knowledge
the worst is before death, there is no discussion or cracks, people are deceived
It seems there's already so much, and fear is endless
the courage of the little mouse calmly scurrying across the fast lane
is greater than ten men

5.

All along I've known I'm a supremely timid person
only comfortable doing safe small things

I've never wanted to change anything
especially the truth inlayed in dense patterns around my head
although it isn't worthy of getting in anyone's way

For a long time, insight has both harmed and helped
never feeling safe, every time I lift my head I see black clouds crossing the sky

I've always worried about being timid
but in the end fear actualizes the body, it smashes right into things
fear is inexplicable, hard objects closer than three centimeters,
that is fear itself

Gradually approaching, the paltry, illiterate, and auspicious are all bundled up
everyone is there, no one makes it out, no one escapes
all people can make is fear

Nobody is innocent, just as nobody is fearless
no one gives up, no one forgives, no one deserves protection
bravery should be reinterpreted, man must realize he's only oppressed by fear
like a northern December, he can only wrap himself up in a thick cotton quilt

一切能摇的，发得出响动的，能被触摸的
这种时候，只有害怕还会怜悯，还不肯放弃我们
它总是反身回来，把准星再订正一遍
望望未来，能看见它给所有所有的，事先加盖了绝对的封印

战战兢兢地我好像逮着了我的真理
现在，我要阖紧了手，不再松开，这下安心了

At a time where everything can be shaken, make faint sounds, be touched,
        only fear still shows pity
it always turns around and resets the gun-sights
facing the future it sees it has provided everything, has already stamped the
        right seal

Trembling with terror, I seem to have captured my truth
now, I'll clasp my hands tightly, never open them again, and for once feel
        at ease

月夜里经过的火车

之一

什么经过，是什么，实在凄凉，实在是沉。
有个家伙长久地在钝物上拖铁索
载火的车，吃的铁，穿的铁，想的铁。

惊坐起来，我四处摸铁索。

之二

大地发白，月亮正在下葬
葬礼拖得无限长。

被那怪物吃进去的赶路者
漫长地忍受这冰凉的晚上一寸寸勒进肉。
大地蹦跳着迎接磨损
光亮就将耗尽，满天轰隆隆的都是黑。

之三

月亮偶然睁开它的三角眼
夜晚翻滚。
正转弯的火车，屁股先亮了
拉满家书的邮政车，晶晶露白骨。

据说骨头不值钱，心情抵万金。

Train Passing Through a Moonlit Night

I.

What is passed by, that's what there is, desolate, silent.
And this thing, forever dragging iron chains over dull things
a train loaded with fire, eating iron, wearing iron, thinking iron.

Sitting up startled, I feel iron chains all around me.

II.

The earth turns white, the moon is being interred
the funeral drags on forever.

The hurrying ones consumed by the monster
endure the endless frigid night that cinches inch by inch into flesh.
The earth jumps to welcome its damage
the light will be used up, everything that rumbles through the sky is black.

III.

The moon happens to open its triangular eye
night churns on.
On the turning train, the caboose lights up first
the mail car stuffed full of letters from home flashes bone.

It's said that bones are worthless, a state of mind is worth millions.

之四

心啊，没什么可喜欢的
只能喜欢夜空背后黑汪汪的深。

火车慌不择路
用力抓紧镶金嵌银的土地
生怕被抛出去，生怕凌空倒坠。
蜈蚣在打滑，四脚朝天，呵呵，就在这淡月夜。

之五

火车，在鬼影下挨家挨户敲玻璃
披白斗篷火车的，一个玩伴也不放过。
谁能跳出这游戏
拒绝和火和铁和过往的自己扭在一起。

时日都不多了。
玻璃里钻出石英，石英正拼命下雪
天下就要大白，嚯，火车都远了
为什么还要四处摸铁索。

IV.

Ah this mind, there is nothing it likes
it can only like the boundless black depths behind the night sky.

The train is too flustered to pick a track
it grasps the gilded silver-inlaid earth
for fear it will be thrown off, or soar up and crash back down.
Centipedes slide about, landing legs in the air, *haha*, in the pale moonlit night.

V.

Under the shadow of ghosts, the train goes door to door knocking on glass
the white-cloaked train doesn't let a single player off.
Who can quit this game
refusals and fire and iron and the self that comes and goes all intertwine.

There isn't much time.
Quartz burrows out from glass, quartz risks its life to make snow.
the world is about to be exposed, all the trains are far away
and why do I still feel iron chains everywhere?

JINTIAN SERIES OF CONTEMPORARY LITERATURE

Flash Cards
Yu Jian
Translated by Wang Ping & Ron Padgett

The Changing Room
Zhai Yongming
Translated by Andrea Lingenfelter

Doubled Shadows
Ouyang Jianghe
Translated by Austin Woerner

A Phone Call from Dalian
Han Dong
Edited by Nicky Harman
Translated by Nicky Harman, Maghiel van Crevel,
Yu Yan Chen, Naikan Tao, Tony Prince & Michael Day

Wind Says
Bai Hua
Translated by Fiona Sze-Lorrain

I Can Almost See the Clouds of Dust
Yu Xiang
Translated by Fiona Sze-Lorrain

Canyon in the Body
Lan Lan
Translated by Fiona Sze-Lorrain